Praise for *Nature's Final Curtain Call?*

"This book is timely and spot-on. These beautiful verses not only cajole but also lure us into an aesthetic relationship with nature. . . . This book calls for our ecological repentance. With enthusiasm, I recommend it to you."

—Young Ho Chun, Saint Paul School of Theology, emeritus

"Why rhyme? Rhyming words together create relationships. We remember sounds that help us predict what will come next. S T's poetry invites us to harmonize with nature, create earthy relationships, and predict the future. His rhymes create a sense of harmony, a kinship with flowers, trees, waves, and breeze. Rhyme can also disrupt those unexamined expectations. The power of the text is in one line: 'What if all nature slowly dies and beauty cannot grace your eyes?'"

—Heather Murray Elkins, Drew Theological School, emerita

"In a poetic extravaganza, scholar, author, musician, pastor, prophet, and global citizen S T Kimbrough evokes memories of nature's exhilarating performances. Will we be sufficiently wonderstruck by creation to prioritize its care? Will we, most invasive of species, awaken to properly tend the Earth from which we are formed? Or will we somnambulate toward our planet's final curtain?"

—Mark Terwilliger, United Methodist Earthkeeper

Nature's Final Curtain Call?

Nature's Final Curtain Call?

Who Cares About Creation's Care?

S T Kimbrough, Jr.

Foreword by Russell E. Richey

RESOURCE *Publications* • Eugene, Oregon

NATURE'S FINAL CURTAIN CALL?
Who Cares About Creation's Care?

Copyright © 2022 S T Kimbrough, Jr. All rights reserved. Except for brief quotations in critical publications or reviews, no part of this book may be reproduced in any manner without prior written permission from the publisher. Write: Permissions, Wipf and Stock Publishers, 199 W. 8th Ave., Suite 3, Eugene, OR 97401.

Resource Publications
An Imprint of Wipf and Stock Publishers
199 W. 8th Ave., Suite 3
Eugene, OR 97401

www.wipfandstock.com

PAPERBACK ISBN: 978-1-6667-3811-7
HARDCOVER ISBN: 978-1-6667-9841-8
EBOOK ISBN: 978-1-6667-9842-5

04/12/22

Contents

Foreword by Russell E. Richey — xi
Introduction — xv

Section 1: Nature's Seasons

1. Seasons — 3
2. Mother Nature's Poetry — 4
3. A Toast to Spring — 5
4. Unforeseen Surprise — 6
5. Big Island, Hawaii — 8
6. Season of Seasons — 9

Section 2: Nature's Weather

7. Nature's Encore — 13
8. Spellbound — 14
9. The Joy of Sunlight — 15
10. Sunlight's New Chance — 16
11. Raindrops — 17
12. Wind and Rain — 18
13. Darkness and Light — 19
14. Fragrant Breezes — 20
15. The Charm and Threat of Water — 21
16. Unexpected Survival — 22
17. On the Rhine — 23
18. Weather Wise? — 24
19. One More Day at the Beach — 25

Section 3: Nature's Flowers

20. A Rose by Light — 29
21. A Single Flower — 30
22. Laughing Flowers — 31
23. Lavender — 32
24. The Silversword — 33
25. Gerber Daisies — 34
26. Hibiscus Blooms — 35
27. Rhododendrons — 36
28. A Four-leaf Clover — 37

Section 4: Nature's Creatures

29. A Bird Duet — 41
30. Duet Continued — 42
31. A Lone Bird's Song — 43
32. A Mockingbird — 44
33. Another Mockingbird — 45
34. A Sparrow Day — 46
35. The Falcon — 47
36. The Wise Wren — 48
37. Gone in a Flash — 49
38. No Show — 50
39. Once in the Maasai Mara — 51
40. A Forest Stroll — 53
41. Butterflies — 54
42. A Menagerie of Birds — 55

Section 5: Nature's Scenes

43. To Step Among the Stars — 59
44. A Trek Up to a Waterfall — 60
45. All the Same — 61
46. Another Morning — 62

47. Nature's Course . . . 63
48. Sea Moods . . . 64
49. The Gobi Desert . . . 65
50. The River Runs . . . 67
51. Wonders of the Beach . . . 68
52. The Beach . . . 70
53. One More Day at the Beach . . . 71
54. Ripples . . . 72
55. Nature's Romance . . . 73
56. Beauty's Shadows . . . 74
57. A Willow Tree . . . 75
58. Nature's Art . . . 76
59. Nature's Prayer Shawl . . . 77
60. Nature's Icons . . . 78
61. Colored Fantasy . . . 79
62. Beauty's Abode . . . 80
63. Nature's Balladeer . . . 81
64. Nighttime Skies . . . 82

Section 6: Nature's Care

65. Caring for Nature . . . 85
66. Nature's Final Curtain Call . . . 87
67. Nature's Misuse . . . 88
68. New Jersey Beaches, Past and Present . . . 90
69. The Holy Ganges? . . . 92
70. Out of Control . . . 93
71. The Earth on Fire . . . 94
72. Though Winter, It's Like Springtime . . . 96
73. Ignorance We Can't Afford . . . 98
74. An Estuary . . . 99
75. "Creation's Care" . . . 100

Foreword

> The morning with sunrise begins,
>   as moon and stars depart.
> The sky a vast blue color wins
>   and birds their courses start.
> . . .
> How interesting that nature cares
>   for me, as I should care
> for nature, yet I create snares
>   that nature can impair.
>
> As morning sunrise and fresh air
>   are nature's gifts to me,
> I pray I will for nature care
>   the way it cares for me:
>
> to stop pollution, fracking too,
>   help neighbors, friends to see
> strip-mining from a different view,
>   rivers pollution free!

In *well-versed verse* S T Kimbrough, Jr., charts the reader's way through the natural world. His poetry charms the reader through six successive sections aptly titled "Nature's . . . *Seasons, Weather, Flowers, Creatures, Scenes,* and *Care*. His moving and descriptive lines in the first five sections invite us into nature. How? Successive poems pilot us near, into, and through what's around us that moves, lives, and presents itself. The very first poem in twelve crisp lines, aptly titled "Seasons," captures all four, singly and together, in a line or two. In each of the first five sections, Kimbrough takes readers into specific natural realms, with inviting titles (note the highly descriptive titles in "Section 3: Nature's

Flowers": "A Rose by Light," "A Single Flower," "Laughing Flowers," "Lavender").

Kimbrough's poetry keeps the reader on the earthly plane—actually or imaginatively looking back, looking around, looking ahead. The religiously-inclined and those familiar with his incredible scholarly and artistic production might expect the attention to move quickly onto a theological level and make claims about divine provisions for humankind. Not here! Not in this collection! Here his *well-versed verse* presumes no religious commitments, views, or interests. To be sure, he uses a few often-theologically-loaded terms—"creation" some sixteen times, "care" thirteen, and the potentially evocative "nature" one hundred and thirty-nine. However, this remarkable and engaging collection invites all to look afresh at the world around us—those disdainful of religion, skeptics, adherents of any religion, sectarians, and ecumenists. That celebrative spirit pushes the reader to glory in the world that we still see, in its various dimensions, actors, or aspects, with verse that invites us into the natural world.

The successive sections recall for Jews and Christians (and all interested parties) the first chapter of scripture. As in Genesis, "Nature's Care" details humanity's original sin! Today's violation? Our "eating" the natural world's "apple" with multiple bites of pollution, strip-mining, global warming, greenhouse gas, oceans of/in plastic waste, over-building, and draining of estuaries. So we—today's Adams and Eves—having lived in the garden of Eden, eaten of every permitted tree and now of the forbidden tree of the knowledge of good and evil, face our expulsion from the garden. Traveling out of Eden and through biblical story after story, readers can/may find encouragement with the long narrative of God's care for us, an often erring people. *Nature's Final Curtain Call? Who Cares About Creation's Care?* takes readers of Kimbrough's first five sections of poetry back to Eden.

"Section 6: Nature's Care," the last, might well have been entitled "Our Uncared-for and Scarred Nature," or "Nature's Looming Doom: Our Doing," or "Coming Disasters for Nature's Seasons, Weather, Flowers, Creatures, Scenes," or, for Jews and Christians,

"Nature's Care: Knowing Good and Evil." In the crisp lines of the section's first poem, "Caring for Nature," quoted above, Kimbrough implicates us all and our leadership in pollution, fracking, and strip-mining. Steadily, verse-by-verse, poem-by-poem, "Nature's Care" takes us—meaning "us" in every political/economic/social realm—into the world we are systematically and steadily destroying. With text, themes, and titles, Kimbrough reminds readers that we are all implicated, if only by inaction, in the systematic destruction of the world. Our sitting through the unfolding drama—rather than jumping onto the stage to intervene—he captures with the book's title, *Nature's Final Curtain Call? Who Cares About Creation's Care?* Strangely, the last section, with its powerful and scary imagery and warnings of the chaotic world to come, enhances the beauty, compelling, and invitational character of the poetry in the first five sections. In welcome and doom, warmth and chill, peace and chaos, and charm and prophecy, Kimbrough's *well-versed verse* certainly lures the reader into a scary world-to-come, but his first five sections might deserve more of an invitation than the collection's title suggests. His introduction, to be sure, addresses the contrasts, but I implore readers of this Foreword to relish—and I'll say it again—the beauty, compelling, and invitational character of the poetry in the first five sections.

Well-versed verse is a Kimbrough trademark. He has a stunning bibliography of a richly varying character which touches various current and enduring issues and topics. How?—in widely ranging historical works, treatises on Charles Wesley, dialogues between Methodist and Orthodox theologians, Eastern European/Russian issues, and biblical studies. Poetry, as well as these scholarly publications, seemingly comes naturally for Kimbrough. For example, without mentioning his extensive bibliography with a number of publishers, the Wipf and Stock catalogue alone includes nine volumes of his poetry as well as a number of scholarly works.

Kimbrough's last poem captures this remarkable collection's tour through nature, relishing in the creation we have been given, and reminding us of the challenge we face in caring for the world around us.

FOREWORD

"Creation's care!" a vital cry:
    caress the earth, the forests, trees.
By no means let the oceans die,
    or bring the isle folk to their knees.

"Creation's care" should now become
    a topic of our daily speech
reminding us how careless, dumb
    to place such care beyond all reach.

"Creation's care," no hopeless task,
    no futile gesture from the left,
our negligence it will unmask,
    lest we're of nature's gifts bereft.

"Creation's care" takes effort, work
    "Creation's care," each day's concern,
no person can afford to shirk.
    "Creation's care" we all must learn.

Here once more Kimbrough's *well-versed verse* is an instructive and rewarding read.

RUSSELL E. RICHEY, Dean Emeritus of Candler School of Theology and William R. Cannon Distinguished Professor of Church History Emeritus; Visiting Professor of Methodism, Duke Divinity School; General Editor, *Methodist Review*

Introduction

In the performing arts, curtain calls transpire when performers return to the stage to be recognized by the audience for their performance. It may seem somewhat strange to speak of "nature's curtain call," but I am thinking of those amazing moments when with the passing of seasons Mother Nature presents a stunning performance, so to speak, for which we, the observers, are amazed: the appearance of spring's flowers, the budding trees of spring, snow-white winter snow, huge flocks of Canadian geese flying south, the filling of dry waterbeds with late spring's melting snow, the stunning colors of autumn's leaves, the glorious colors of desert flowers, newborn animals of diverse species, and changing climates across the earth. There are cycles of nature that enable these wonders.

The poems in this book address some of the wonders of nature: the seasons, weather, flowers, creatures, and beautiful scenes of nature. In the final section, however, the question is raised as to whether the wonders will survive the devastating effects of climate change and other threats to nature. Will humankind awaken to the need of caring for nature? One poem expresses this need somewhat differently: Could it be that we may be experiencing "Nature's Final Curtain Call"?

> If wonder, beauty are not there
> and nature's splendors we can't share,
> with awe stripped from the human soul,
> what will be left to make us whole?

First, however, it is important to celebrate some of the wonders of nature all around us (Section 1) each day so that we might be fully aware of what is at stake when it comes to the demise of nature. Mother Nature has her own poetry, which she shares with us daily around the world.

> The tree limbs long and intertwined,
>   like figures of geometry,
> as though an artist they'd designed
>   are Mother Nature's poetry.

There is something in the change and rhythm of seasons that awakes in us diverse emotions of calm, ecstasy, joy, and surprise.

> O springtime, now I raise my glass
>   to toast the beauty that you bring
> to everyone who here will pass.
>   You give each heart a song to sing.
> . . .
> The soft trade winds soothe spirit, mind,
>   as does the hush of waves.
> Hawaii is one of a kind
>   for which the spirit craves.
> . . .
> High up on the volcanic slopes
>   there snow's a rare delight;
> on beaches waves give surfers hopes
>   of long rides left and right.

Winter brings snow and trappers' challenges in the Yukon. There is a spawning season for salmon in the northwest, and whales return to the Pacific waters of the west seeking to harvest krill for nourishment. Bears come out of hibernation to renewed life in the wild. And as the sap rises in the maple trees of the north, syrup fills buckets with a delicious addition to various cuisines.

Section 2 treats the wonders and dangers of weather across the world. We are struck with awe and fear as various weather patterns shift.

> The snowflakes fly down from its limbs
>   and sparkle on the ground,
> and winds resound with forest hymns,
>   a moment I'm spellbound.

INTRODUCTION

Wherever we turn there are the joys and fears of sunlight. We cannot imagine life without sun and water, yet we fear the dangers their excess and lack often bring.

> Torrential rains can flood a plain
> where water finds no place to drain.
> Yet without raindrops comes a drought
> and life is lost with no way out.

At other times it seems that rain is the source of wondrous music.

> The raindrops play such a sweet tune
> on tin roofs seen nearby;
> it sounds a bit like "Claire de Lune"
> or gentle lullaby.

The weather can bring delight and joy, but it can also bring tsunamis, destruction, and death. The history of violent storms of devastation reveals the horrific results of the worst of Mother Nature's trying power. Yet now global warming increases the frequency and intensity of such storms.

> As global warming makes storms worse,
> It more and more becomes a curse,
> a curse from which there's scarce relief,
> if facts of science shape belief.
> If not, the world is surely doomed,
> for its disasters we'll have groomed.

When we think of the loss of earth's beauties because of global warming, we think immediately of nature's flowers (Section 3). Imagine that parched earth can no longer nurture the seeds that bring forth a hillside of heather in spring, a meadow of lavender, a rose for a loved one. Each type of flower has its own unique scent, each stem and petal have their own character. And oh, thousands of colors fill nature's forests and fields.

INTRODUCTION

> The earth laughs through its flowers,
> when nurtured by spring showers.
> Their blooms reveal they're smiling
> with colors most beguiling.
> The colors are caressing
> the beauty they're expressing.

Shall we not preserve these amazing sources of beauty that give life reason to be?

Nature not only fills our eyes with amazing and inspiring sights; it provides a menagerie of creatures (Section 4), especially birds who thrill us with their delightful songs.

> The constant song of one lone bird,
> when not another one is heard,
> fills forests, hillsides, fields around
> with melody and winsome sound.
> . . .
> A nightingale, a meadowlark
> will sing at daylight or at dark.

Nature also gifts us with the graceful flights of "The Falcon" and "Butterflies," the swiftness of rabbits and foxes ("Gone in a Flash"), and the amazing and innumerable animals of the African plains ("Once in the Masaai Mara"): wildebeests, lions, giraffes, hippopotami, antelopes, gazelles, hyenas. The diversity of nature's creatures is immense. They are not only majestic creatures in their own right; they are also sources of food and sustenance.

> These animals are all a gift
>   to each other, humankind.
> Their beauty gives us all a lift,
>   and never should be maligned.
>
> Protect them for the years to come
>   from hunters, poachers, and greed.
> Some to extinction will succumb,
>   if we do not heed this need.

The space age has extended our concepts of nature far beyond the boundaries of earth and its atmosphere.

INTRODUCTION

>If I could step among the stars
>>Orion, Leo, Milky Way,
>far, far away from streets and cars,
>>I'd gather up my own bouquet
>of stardust from a galaxy
>>no telescope has viewed before,
>so far beyond reality
>>where only shooting stars can soar.

As we reflect on the scenes of nature (Section 5) that surround our daily lives, they seem to embrace us with comfort and discomfort each day ("Nature's Course").

>And so begins another day
>>of nature's thrilling course of change,
>where white clouds swiftly turn to gray,
>>or stormy ones, threatening, strange.

Nature's diverse scenes fill us with awe, wonder, as well as anguish. There is the utter joy of "A Trek Up to a Waterfall," the majesty of the sea ("Sea Moods"), the marvelous expanse of "The Gobi Desert," the "Wonders of the Beach," and the enchantment of rivers and streams. Yet the question haunts us: Could these natural wonders be lost?

So much in nature seems to conform to cycles of repetition ("All the Same"): the departure and return of seasons, the migration of Wildebeests, the rise and descent of the sun, the nightly return of the moon.

>We think we see nature's sameness,
>but what seems the same is never so.
>. . .
>Each year cranes return to the same lakes,
>sea turtles bury their eggs on the same beach.
>We are born, we grow, we live, we die,
>just the same as everyone before us:
>all the same, yet never the same.

Nature's scenes so often affect our moods ("Sea Moods") and emotions. Our attitudes toward a day before us are often shaped by nature.

INTRODUCTION

> What solace there is in low tide,
> > what comfort in the rhythmic waves,
> what thrill it is to live beside
> > the sea, whose mood my spirit saves!
>
> . . .
>
> I walk along the beach in awe
> > of waves' sleek ever-changing art,
> which artists seek to paint and draw,
> > here Canaletto had his start.

Nature is the source of fear and anguish through fierce storms and erupting volcanoes that can take life away in moments. And yet, nature's wondrous scenes far exceed her threats of disaster ("Nature's Romance").

> These wondrous trees surround the lake;
> > their regal limbs sway, dance.
> And in these moments I partake
> > of nature's charmed romance.

Unfortunately we live in an age that gravely threatens nature ("Nature's Care" Section 6) and its wonders. There is a struggle

> > to stop pollution, fracking too,
> > > help neighbors, friends to see
> > strip-mining from a different view,
> > > rivers pollution free.

Could it be that future generations will experience "Nature's Final Curtain Call"?

> What if all nature slowly dies
> and beauty cannot grace your eyes?
> What if the rivers overrun
> with damage in the millions done?
>
> . . .
>
> The barrenness around the globe
> would seem to be death's shroud or robe.
> What will then humankind befall
> at nature's final curtain call?

"Nature's Misuse" in many arenas is "Out of Control."

INTRODUCTION

> If winter storms come in the fall,
> it seems there's no control at all.
> If summer storms come in the spring,
> tornadoes wipe out everything.
> Sea water's warmer by degrees
> and winds entire towns swiftly seize.
> With fossil fuels oceans rise,
> and island nature slowly dies.

What has happened to human care of creation? Is it completely dead? Can we be awakened?

> Creation's care's no hopeless task,
>   no futile gesture from the left.
> Our negligence it will unmask,
>   lest we're of nature's gifts bereft.

S T Kimbrough Jr.

Section 1

Nature's Seasons

1. Seasons

It's autumn here and springtime there,
while flowers bloom, there trees are bare.
The season contrasts do astound;
the blooms on trees, snow on the ground.
With wintertime there comes a freeze,
with summertime an ocean breeze.
In autumn leaves turn colors bright,
the springtime flowers, what a sight!
The seasons come and seasons go
and oh what joy that it is so.
The summer, autumn, winter, spring
are Mother Nature's choice offspring.

2. Mother Nature's Poetry

The tree limbs long and intertwined,
    like figures of geometry,
as though an artist they'd designed,
    are Mother Nature's poetry.

Soon tiny buds on each tree limb
    will open as green leaves appear.
Then summer winds will sound the hymn
    a forest sings from year to year.

The geometric figures all
    of limbs that are so intertwined
are lost from view until the fall
    as nature's seasons are aligned.

3. A Toast to Spring

In spring I wish for flower blooms
    that fill the hillsides with delight.
Their fragrance that hillsides perfumes
    across the meadows soon takes flight.

It wafts o'er hillsides, meadows, streams,
    a field where there's a flowing brook,
where daffodils, as if in dreams,
    fill up the banks where'er you look.

O, Springtime, now I raise my glass
    to toast the beauty that you bring
to everyone who here will pass.
    You give each heart a song to sing.

4. Unforeseen Surprise

The love of nature often saves
    a day I might have lost.
The glistening sand and tumbling waves,
    even winter's first, cold frost
can make the dormant spirit rise
to heights of unforeseen surprise.

With winter comes the sparkling snow
    that shapes a fairyland
of ice cycles' delightful show
    as Mother Nature planned.
The cold of winter makes me yearn
for spring and summer's quick return.

With springtime as the flowers bloom
    my heart with wonder fills.
For hillsides, Mother Nature's room,
    burst forth with color thrills.
The flowers red, blue, white, and green
across the hillsides may be seen.

With summer I'm off to the shore
    to breathe the sea-fresh air,
to hear the waves splash, roar and roar,
    and watch the seagulls dare

to go a-fishing with dispatch
and dive another fish to catch.

With autumn-time the leaves turn, fall,
    and different hues I see.
Fall colors like spring colors all
    are wonders come to be.
A forest stroll in autumn-time
is Mother Nature's time sublime!

5. Big Island, Hawaii

Some say Hawaii is just so:
    there thrives a soft, warm breeze.
And yet these islands storms well know,
    that make life ill at ease.

Big Island also claims to span
    ten major climate zones
with little more amazing than
    its miles of lava cones.

High up on the volcanic slopes
    there snow's a rare delight;
on beaches waves give surfers hopes
    of long rides left and right.

Some summer days are dry, cool, warm,
    there're even desert climes,
but tropical monsoons can harm,
    and yet there're pleasant times.

The soft trade winds soothe spirit, mind,
    as does the hush of waves.
Hawaii is one of a kind
    for which the spirit craves.

6. Season of Seasons

Across the earth at Easter time
    one senses Mother Earth would sing
and wonders bring to every clime
    in summer, autumn, winter, spring.

For Easter, God the time has set
    so all creation is reborn.
Though seasons change, lest one forget
    first comes the blade, the ear, the corn.

A desert flower peaks through sand,
    an iceberg floats along the sea.
Siberian farmers till the land,
    a northern woodsman fells a tree.

As Easter comes, returns each year,
    rebirth is its creative theme.
What greater message can we hear:
    God comes creation to redeem?

Section 2

Nature's Weather

7. Nature's Encore

This morning I awoke to ice
    and to a dust of snow.
It made me ponder and think twice—
    Should I my walk forego?

Just then I looked up at the trees
    as sunlight made them shine;
the ice each branch in time did freeze,
    the oak trees, elm, and pine.

It seemed a moment all stood still,
    as I took in the scene,
and then a lonely whippoorwill
    sang clearly, though unseen.

It seemed as though this was its call
    to me, "Come, walk in snow.
O how enchanting is snowfall.
    Do not your walk forego."

I put on hat and gloves, a shawl,
    and stepped outside my door.
Just then came nature's curtain call:
    more snow, nature's encore!

8. Spellbound

As tree limbs do an arabesque
    with wind and snow at play,
one pine tree's shape is quite grotesque,
    its trunk in constant sway.

A giant oak tree stalwart stands,
    as if winds to defy.
Its branches wave like giant hands
    to bid the snow goodbye.

The snowflakes fly down from its limbs
    and sparkle on the ground,
and winds resound with forest hymns,
    a moment I'm spellbound!

9. The Joy of Sunlight

The sun shines brightly, brilliantly,
    though sometimes by clouds it is dimmed,
but I have noticed recently
    it's circled and by blue sky trimmed.

I much prefer a blue-trimmed sun
    than angry clouds, thund'rous and dark.
Each dawn when a new day's begun,
    I'd rather hear a meadowlark.

When morning sun is trimmed with blue
    one hears a chorus of the birds.
When they don't sing, how very true
    I sigh and struggle to find words,

some words to cheer me on my way
    because of dreary weather signs.
But maybe at least one sun ray
    will peak through clouds with blue designs.

When sun rays warm the earth and trees,
    the birds then sing delightful songs.
Like gentle waves of summer seas,
    joy rushes in, the thrill prolongs.

10. Sunlight's New Chance

The green leaves glisten in sunlight
    and wave from winds light touch.
A forest glade blooms with delight,
    wild flowers I love so much.

The morning mist long since is past,
    and every forest scene
yields colors which delight, forecast
    the different shades of green.

At meadow's edge some yellow bright
    sunflowers cast a glow
on blooms of Queen Anne's Lace's white
    which look like fallen snow.

And just beyond strawberry fields
    are cloaked in red and green.
Since nothing from the sunlight shields,
    they cast a sparkling sheen.

Their sheen from sunlight's rays of gold
    joins in the sunlight's dance,
which nature will at dawn remold
    into sunlight's new chance.

11. Raindrops

A single raindrop strikes the ground;
it dissipates and can't be found.
A raindrop I can't see descend,
for raindrops easily can blend
with fields of grass or with gray skies,
and soon they're vanished from my eyes.
Raindrops are born among the clouds
quite far away from maddening crowds.
They water crops, make flowers grow,
with sunlight form a bright rainbow.
They're nature's own life-giving art,
but nature's plans they can outsmart.
Torrential rains can flood a plain
where water finds no place to drain.
Yet without raindrops comes a drought
and life is lost with no way out.
So, raindrops, be our welcome guest;
without you, life cannot be blessed.

12. Wind and Rain

The rain drops play such a sweet tune
    on tin roofs seen nearby;
it sounds a bit like "Claire de Lune"
    or gentle lullaby.

How constant is the steady beat
    of rain drops that descend;
I hear them sound and then repeat,
    it's Mother Nature's trend.

When we've no raindrops, there's the wind
    that whistles through the trees
sweet melodies that often send
    their music as they please.

The music of the wind and rain
    accompanies each day,
and we can hear, so clear and plain,
    that nature is at play.

13. Darkness and Light

Where darkness reigns hope's light grows dim
and vanished the moon's crystal rim,
when nature's storms with terror reign,
an ice storm or a hurricane,
one thinks that all there is, is dark;
there is no light, not even a spark.
One curses scornfully the dark,
depression rises, bold and stark.
And yet the dark cannot endure,
this nature daily does ensure,
for after darkness comes the dawn
and gives us hope to carry on.
This metaphor of night and day
is Mother Nature's way to say:
The dark's replaced by morning light:
a life-scheme filled with keen insight.

14. Fragrant Breezes

The honeysuckle-perfumed air
    recalls an oriental night
when jasmine blooms beyond compare
    sent fragrant breezes of delight
across the lake I sat beside.
    The breezes whispered through the trees
a melody that laid aside
    my earthly cares with utmost ease.

As if transported far away,
    I lingered, drinking in the air.
The breezes led me not astray,
    but turned my thoughts to memories fair
of someone whose bright countenance
    once captured all my heart and soul.
And with a solitary glance
    I sensed that love was in control.

15. The Charm and Threat of Water

At eight o'clock there's snowfall,
    at ten o'clock there's rain,
at one o'clock a sea squall.
    Where can the water drain?

The sea has lost its shoreline,
    the river overflows,
and you can't see the squall line
    as flood waters enclose . . .

enclose our little village
    till there's no place to go,
and river, sea, flood spillage
    becomes the village foe.

It takes a week of waiting
    for waters to subside.
The wait is so frustrating
    in spite of all we've tried.

Still I'll not dare move away
    for water thrills my soul
with highs and lows day by day,
    my soul it can console.

16. Unexpected Survival

A giant whale arching its tail
    burst from the water's deep,
just as a sloop had hoist its sail
    to set a course to keep.

The sloop, so near the cresting whale,
    was rocked from stem to stern.
And as it righted came a gale,
    that forced a dangerous turn.

As if a whirling, maelstrom force
    now strained the sloop to wreck
and thrust it from its long-sought course,
    the water filled the deck.

The crew with all its might held fast
    the sail, lest they might flip;
one braced himself against the mast,
    the rest tightened their grip.

And suddenly the wind was still,
    the water like a lake,
and they could steer the sloop at will,
    for there was scarce a wake.

17. On the Rhine

A gray day dawns upon the Rhine;
I fear it could my mood define.
Quite tricky here weather can be.
If this you doubt, just come and see.

So many days the sky is gray,
and if the sun comes out, hurray!
The streets are suddenly all filled;
the population is so thrilled.

They sit outside at street cafés,
and every child with a friend plays.
One sees how weather changes moods
for on gray days one often broods.

I've lived here long enough to know
that weather should not make life so,
that it controls your attitudes,
at least that's what my mind concludes.

18. Weather Wise?

The sky is gray, the air is warm,
a coming storm could do grave harm.
The birds from trees have flown away;
they're looking for a place to stay,
where they'll be safe from wind and rain,
and they can rest until both wane.
The calm before a storm I fear
is telling me a storm is near.
I'll find a safe place if I'm wise,
for hurricanes have no disguise.
There was a tragic one last year
whose churning winds filled me with fear.
Whole houses from foundations torn,
left families only to mourn.
As global warming makes storms worse,
it more and more becomes a curse,
a curse from which there is relief,
if facts of science shape belief.
If not, the world is surely doomed,
for its disasters we'll have groomed.

19. One More Day at the Beach

The rooftops now are trimmed with blue
    since skies cleared of dark clouds.
I watched the sparrows as they flew
    above the cheering crowds.
They cheered because the rain was gone:
    "Let's go back to the beach."
With all the stormy clouds withdrawn,
    beach fun was within reach.

But some forgot that clouds so dark
    forebode oft stormy seas,
and lifeguards had just seen a shark
    which swimmers did not please.
So, now they spread their towels out
    to lie down and relax.
It's certainly without a doubt,
    they thus missed shark attacks.

Section 3

Nature's Flowers

20. A Rose by Light

The rose I saw by morning light
    supported by a tiny stem
has given me such sheer delight,
    another Mother Nature gem.

Its rose-red color in sun rays
    cast here and there a mystic spell.
It tints the grass as the light plays
    a game I've come to know so well.

It were as though to shadowbox
    all nature through sunlight has learned,
and yet at night moves like a fox;
    the light is gone just as I turned.

Then there arose the round-faced moon
    that plays with shadows and light too,
but morning light can't come too soon
    to bring the red rose into view.

21. A Single Flower

The beauty of a single flower,
    its blooms dressed red and blue,
is sparkling as drops from a shower
    refract the sun's orange hue.

One has to pause amid the rain
    to view this nature art.
a lovely, varied color skein
    that beauty sets apart,

apart it sets this art in time,
    which rarely will repeat.
These raindrop colors in their prime
    become my springtime treat.

22. Laughing Flowers

The earth laughs through its flowers,
when nurtured by spring showers.
Their blooms reveal they're smiling
with colors most beguiling.
The colors are caressing
the beauty they're expressing.
Oh, what a joy is springtime
from early dawn till nighttime.
I love the laughing flowers
that cheer me by the hours.

23. Lavender

One quiet dawn I plucked a stem
    of lavender in a dense grove
where lavender glowed like a gem
    as sunlight struck this treasure-trove.

Its heaven-scented, perfume smell
    transported me beyond all time,
creating such a magic spell,
    the queen of odors, how sublime.

How can a waft of perfumed flowers
    possess at once the human sense
of smell with such enchanting powers
    like those of Orient's incense?

That stem of lavender I've kept
    now pressed within a sacred book,
so I'll remember where I stepped,
    the piece of lavender I took.

24. The Silversword

The silversword's a unique flower
    and only in Hawaii grows.
It has amazing staying power,
    as each Hawaiian knows.

Between September and July
    Hawaii is its only home.
It's red at first, we don't know why,
    but turns then to a muted chrome.

Big Island, Maui, this bloom share,
    for nowhere else can it be found.
The silversword, exquisite, rare,
    with stunning beauty it is crowned.

25. Gerber Daisies

This summer when my daisies bloomed,
a happy sight: colors consumed
my garden with delightful hues
of reds, greens, yellows, whites, and blues.
The regal posture of their stems
held high their petals like large gems.
The sunlight made them sparkling bright
until the sunset brought the night.
I offered then a silent prayer:
I'm thankful for the daisies there.

26. Hibiscus Blooms

A large hibiscus bloom in pink
    is marvelously displayed.
And once again I pause to think
    of beauty that is made,
is made in Mother Nature's course
    of life-sustaining powers,
for she gives birth and is the source
    of multi-colored flowers.

The pink hibiscus that I see,
    why is it pink, not red?
How strange near a large peony
    in the same flower bed,
there stands another regal plant;
    yes, an hibiscus too,
and just as lovely, I will grant,
    though it's another hue.

27. Rhododendrons

The rhododendrons dormant lie
    awaiting buds to form.
It is as if the branches sigh,
    "Bloom, whether cold or warm."

And so, in autumn, winter, spring
    the buds burst forth with cheer.
They multi-colored magic bring;
    they're never timid year on year.

The blooms are part of nature's skein
    of rainbow-colored arts,
which inspiration, joy contain,
    each year with a fresh start.

28. A Four-leaf Clover

When I was young, I thought it so—
    if four-leaf clovers could be found,
good luck they would on me bestow,
    but four-leaf clovers don't abound.

I'd search and search a clover patch,
    not even one of them to find.
I could not find a four-leaf match.
    I thought, "Good luck is in a bind."

And then one day, lo and behold,
    between my fingers there one was.
Had I some secret then been told
    by the famed Wizard, come from Oz?

Yet this I learned, I know it's true,
    this is the luck it really brings:
the four-leaf clover has found you!
    That's luck! That's why my spirit sings.

Section 4

Nature's Creatures

29. A Bird Duet

Two birds are serenading
    a different refrain,
and both are quite persuading
    though one is quaint, one plain.

One soars the scale A to E,
    the other D, E, F,
and it's very clear to me
    they're not in the bass clef.

One chirps, the other answers
    in tones known as birdsong
with music for young dancers,
    to dance the whole day long.

30. Duet Continued

Birds still are serenading.
    Did they sing through the night?
Well, as the day was fading
    I heard them with delight.

Perhaps tonight I'll listen,
    after the sun has set,
to hear if their tones glisten
    like Mozart's allegrett'.

31. A Lone Bird's Song

The constant song of one lone bird,
when not another one is heard,
fills forests, hillsides, fields around,
with melody and winsome sound:
a solo nature serenade,
a concert beautifully made.
The harmony of nature's art,
creation's music of the heart.
If you will pause and tune your ear,
you'll be surprised what you will hear.
A nightingale, a meadowlark
will sing at daylight or at dark.
A waterfall, a brook, a stream
supply the rhythms that all seem
accompaniments beyond compare,
as we in nature's music share.

32. A Mockingbird

Last night I heard a mockingbird,
    at least I thought 'twas so,
but then I thought the sound I heard
    might have come from a crow.

A mockingbird that makes the sound
    of squawking like a crow
can quickly change its call around
    to bird songs that you know.

A sparrow's chirp, a red bird's song,
    a wren's sweet, sleek refrain,
one bird can nature's joy prolong
    again and yet again.

33. Another Mockingbird

A mockingbird now sings a song
    from my wide window sill.
It sings and sings the morning long
    as it displays its skill.

It sounds just like a squawking crow
    and then a cooing dove,
and then a song I did not know,
    I think—a song of love.

A raven, robin, pigeon, owl,
    what song will it sing next?
A seagull or some other fowl—
    so many, I'm perplexed!

34. A Sparrow Day

The wind blows softly in the trees,
    the limbs in rhythm sway.
The summer sun rays warmly please,
    while sparrows sing and play.

High in the trees they've built a nest,
    where little ones were born.
And now grown sparrows have no rest
    till they find food each morn.

The hungry little sparrows wait
    for nourishment each day,
till each one hunger can abate
    with Mom and Pop's buffet,

buffet of insects, worms, and seeds,
    fit for these little ones,
will fill their appetites and needs
    till each one flies and runs.

35. The Falcon

To see a daring falcon's flight,
    it soar with graceful ease,
can thrill us with such rare delight,
    that humans can't reprise,

reprise the elegance and grace
    the swift turns, dips, and dives;
the art each falcon paints in space,
    that on wind currents thrives.

Yes, we've machines that soar through space
    and break through ev'n Mach 3,
but falcons they cannot displace;
    they cannot fly carefree.

In nature all is not carefree;
    there's order, there's design,
and falcons are what they're to be,
    for wings falcons define.

A falcon soars where'er it will,
    carefree or with intent
to capture food for its own fill,
    or float as if content.

36. The Wise Wren

A tiny wren peeked out the door
    of its fine birdhouse dwelling.
Should it stay put or go explore?
    Which is the more compelling?

What hungry chirps one hears within,
    the newborn wrens are singing:
"Hey, Papa Wren, your quest begin.
    It's time you're breakfast bringing."

Just as he perched to fly away
    to find their morning repast,
he saw a cat, to his dismay,
    intent to find its breakfast.

The papa wren thought best to wait
    until this threat subsided,
or else for sure he'd be the bait,
    that food the cat provided.

37. Gone in a Flash

A rabbit skipped across my lawn
just as the sun peeked through at dawn.

It scampered quickly to a tree
right where a chipmunk stood carefree.

The rabbit stopped right in its tracks,
no single joint did it relax.

The chipmunk stared, as it stood still;
the rabbit seemed to have a chill.

Though frozen still, a lightning crash
so scared them, both left in a flash!

38. No Show

A red fox strutted down the street,
    as I sat rocking in a swing.
What was its goal, something to eat?
    If so, it did not find a thing.

He should have come by yesterday
    because a rabbit jumped right out
from bushes where it liked to play,
    and I'd have seen a chase, no doubt.

But can a red fox be that fast—
    to catch a rabbit on the run?
Another question to be asked:
    Will fox or rabbit be outdone?

Well, I'll be here tomorrow too,
    perhaps again I'll sit and swing
and see what creatures come in view
    or if I'll just a ditty sing.

39. Once in the Maasai Mara[1]

In Kenya's Maasai Mara's plains
    I've lions, elephants seen,
and many animal domains
    like lakes where hippos convene.

And once I saw the wildebeests
    migrating in a long line,
but broken by some lion feasts,
    when they on wildebeests dine.

At breakfast at a lodge one day
    some stately giraffes passed by.
They were not looking for new prey
    but fresh tree leaves hanging high.

And then there was a great surprise—
    a baby elephant passed.
There seemed to be fear in its eyes.
    Where was its mother? I asked.

---

1. Maasai Mara, sometimes it is spelled Masai Mara. It is a large national game reserve in Narok, Kenya, which joins with the Serengeti National Park in Tanzania. It is named for the Maasai people, whose ancestors lived in the area. "Mara" means "spotted" in the Maasai language. The name comes from the short bushy trees spread across the landscape, which appear as spots when viewed from afar.

I hope the mother was not prey
    to some mean poacher's long bow.
This danger does not go away,
    though those opposed seem to grow.

These animals are nature's gift
    to each other, humankind.
Their beauty gives us all a lift,
    and never should be maligned.

Protect them for the years to come
    from hunters, poachers, and greed.
Some to extinction will succumb,
    if we do not heed this need.

40. A Forest Stroll

A forest stroll has saved a day,
    which seemed at daybreak bleak.
The sun which scarcely cast a ray
    was playing hide and seek.
Just then a cheerful whippoorwill
    broke into winsome song.
Its charming and melodious skill
    is why I skip along.

41. Butterflies

The butterflies fly here and there
    with wings of yellow, blue, and red.
My butterfly bush is not bare,
    and that's where they are daily fed.

The butterfly bush blooms are sweet
    in taste and in their fragrance too.
The butterflies find them a treat,
    so fluttering they wait in queue.

I sit and watch them with delight,
    and when their colors come in view,
I think, oh what a glorious sight,
    creation's color, hue on hue.

42. A Menagerie of Birds

I saw a cardinal alight
    a limb where there's a bluebird nest.
Just then a goldfinch came in sight
    near where some blackbirds came to rest.
Menagerie of colors bright:
    there's red and gold and blue and black,
not one of them had taken flight.
    What birds of color do I lack?

Perhaps if there were a white swan,
    or a blue heron flying by,
and I could wave a magic wand,
    I'd see a cockatoo and sigh.
What an array of colored birds
    grace nature's multi-colored frame.
No matter how I choose my words,
    I'm lost such beauty to exclaim.

Section 5

Nature's Scenes

43. To Step Among the Stars

If I could step among the stars
    Orion, Leo, Milky Way,
far, far away from streets and cars,
    I'd gather up my own bouquet
of stardust from a galaxy
    no telescope has viewed before,
so far beyond reality
    where only shooting stars can soar.

I'd tip my hat to Mr. Moon
    and give a wave to Hercules;
I'd marvel at the wonders strewn,
    across the heavens like Pisces.
And if I passed by Pluto, Mars,
    I simply would not comprehend
the vastness of the realm of stars—
    a realm with no apparent end.

44. A Trek Up to a Waterfall

Ascending to a waterfall
    that's on a mountain side,
at times I feel I face a wall
    without a place to hide.
I'm out of breath, my muscles ache,
    I sit and rest awhile.
My body's tiring, I can't fake
    my former teenage style.

Okay, I need the muscle tone
    that walking helps me find.
Fatigue at my age grasps each bone
    as I try to unwind.
Along the way some giant rocks
    provide a place to sit.
Take off my shoes and then my socks,
    get out my first-aid kit.

A tube of soothing, cool foot balm
    I use, massage my feet.
My heavy breathing now is calm,
    a health bar is my treat.
So, on I go and climb some more
    till finally I am there.
I could not know what was in store:
    a waterfall quite rare.

45. All the Same

Silk-coated clouds on breaths of blue
float softly on gentle puffs of wind,
while geese fly south in annual tableau
of nature's artistic, stunning skill.
Year by year, canvas by canvas,
painters try to capture the scene,
always the same, yet always different.
We think we see nature's sameness,
but what seems the same is never so.
The annual migration of wildebeests,
is it not at the same time, on the same route?
Little ones, the look-a-likes, have grown,
older ones died, others were a lion's meal.
Each year cranes return to the same lakes,
sea turtles bury their eggs on the same beach.
We are born, we grow, we live, we die,
just the same as everyone before us:
all the same, yet never the same.

46. Another Morning

As sunlight beams across my room,
    I gaze at green trees and blue skies.
A neighbor starts his shrubs to groom,
    a squirrel through a window spies.
A breeze wafts through my open door
    and all around begins the day,
and I must soon begin a chore,
    but then I see a large blue jay.

My window sill it makes its perch.
    and striking a proud, regal pose,
it peers my way as if to search,
    then suddenly away it goes.
So goes my early morning time.
    How fortunate I am to be
in such a pleasant, sunny clime
    and pleased with nature to agree.

47. Nature's Course

The ocean waters colored blue
    are compliments to dark blue skies.
The shoreline grass sparkles with dew
    just as the sun begins to rise.

The moonbeams on the water fade,
    as clouds are pierced by bright sunlight.
The water color turns to jade;
    the dew on shoreline grass takes flight.

And so, begins another day
    of nature's thrilling course of change,
where white clouds swiftly turn to gray,
    or stormy ones, threatening, strange.

In contrast there's the ocean calm
    with scarce a sound that can be heard,
except for gentle, wavelike balm
    by which one's soul is calmly stirred.

48. Sea Moods

I'm walking on the beach today,
    where once I lived for many years.
At early morn the ocean spray
    refreshes me as dawn appears.
A walk with sand beneath my feet
    and fading stars above my head—
what better way the day to greet
    instead of lying in my bed?

I saw a sand crab flit along,
    a school of dolphins crest and dive;
I heard a noisy seagull throng;
    oh, how these sea-bound birds do thrive!
But my attention quickly turned
    to sunrise and its golden light;
from sunrise I for years have learned
    to hope, for dawn comes after night.

Each step I took evoked recall
    of happy hours spent by the sea
in winter, springtime, summer, fall,
    for where else would I rather be?
What solace there is in low tide,
    what comfort in the rhythmic waves,
what thrill it is to live beside
    the sea, whose moods my spirit saves!

49. The Gobi Desert

I saw the Gobi Desert's vast
    expanse of glowing sand;
mirage upon mirage was cast
    across this charming land.

The long horizon in the sun
    was clear for miles to see,
where blue sky seemed to run and run
    as if it were the sea.

I stood and gazed with sheer delight
    and longed one thing to see:
the desert flowers one may sight
    if rain should chance to be.

Alas, there was no rain that day,
    it's such a rarity,
and when the sun faded away,
    one thing was clear to me:

The temperature had dropped so fast
    that soon the desert cold
was such a desperate contrast,
    as often I'd been told.

I marveled at the beaming moon,
    the clarity of stars,
retreated to a *ger*² quite soon
    where warmth the coldness bars.

---

2. A Mongolian *ger* is a traditional round-shaped dwelling used by Mongols since they began nomadic life with animal husbandry. It is their home or dwelling and is portable so that it can be moved from place to place as weather and animal care require.

50. The River Runs

The river runs, and runs, and runs;
its tributaries, little ones,
join in the stream that's rushing by,
and fill the riverbed, once dry.
With melting snow and springtime's rain
the river flows and's full again.
Across the river on the shore
a youngster's fishing there once more.
His father helps him bait the hook
and hopes for catfish Mom will cook.
The river runs, and runs, and runs
for fathers fishing with their sons.

51. Wonders of the Beach

As thousands of fine grains of sand
    beam sparkles from a sunlit glow,
one does not know where they may land,
    to paradise they seem to go.

A paradise of sparkling beams
    across the sandy beach I've seen.
This is the stuff that makes up dreams.
    Indeed, in paradise I've been.

In daytime's light the sand reveals
    such wonders one can't see at night.
A glance the sea-glass quickly steals,
    as do sea shells that come in sight.

I walk along the beach in awe
    of waves' sleek, ever-changing art,
which artists seek to paint and draw;
    here Canaletto had his start.

The water's beauty can entice
    the artist's skill to start again
to capture images precise
    or less precise that entertain.

Some make one feel the water's near,
> while some create an atmosphere,
impressions that may be less clear,
> the unforeseen then may appear.

The beach with wonders unforeseen
> entices one: return, return.
You'll know the place where you have been
> to be the place for which you yearn.

52. The Beach

The sky is cloudy, overcast,
    and scarcely is one seen;
the beach's emptiness is vast,
    amazingly serene.

The word serenity says all,
    all that one needs to say.
The calm at morning or nightfall
    gives peace throughout the day.

53. One More Day at the Beach

The rooftops now are trimmed with blue
    since skies cleared of dark clouds.
I watched the sparrows as they flew
    above the cheering crowds.
They cheered because the rain was gone;
    "Let's go back to the beach."
With all the stormy clouds withdrawn,
    beach fun was within reach.

But some forgot that clouds so dark
    forebode sometimes rough seas.
Just then they heard lifeguards remark,
    "With winds as strong as these
we'll put up quickly the red flag!"
    This means—No swimming now!
They put their togs back in a bag;
    they'll swim when times allow.

54. Ripples

The water ripples on the bay,
    no one of them alike.
They twist this way and turn that way,
    a few the shore will strike.

All water ripples are unique;
    they're here and then they're gone.
Each ripple has its own mystique,
    worthwhile to think upon.

Just toss a stone into a lake
    and watch the ripples grow.
Their cue they from the center take
    as they all outward go.

Life's like a ripple, to be sure;
    it's here and then it's gone.
Each ripple has its own allure,
    worthwhile to think upon.

55. Nature's Romance

As night falls on a mountain lake
    the moonlight softly glows
and casts a spell until daybreak,
    that gentle waves expose.

The moonlight captures each wave's edge,
    that in another folds,
then disappears into the sedge
    that on the shoreline holds.

At daybreak moonlight disappears;
    its magic spell is gone.
And sunlight's hazy mist then clears
    to greet the newborn dawn.

The birds awaken from night roosts;
    the animals now stir.
As darkness quickly is reduced,
    I see the Douglas fir.

These wondrous trees surround the lake;
    their regal limbs sway, dance.
And in these moments I partake
    of nature's charmed romance.

56. Beauty's Shadows

When beauty's shadows can't be seen,
and they're not cast across the scene,
the atmosphere is blank and dark,
one hears not ev'n a meadowlark.
When beauty's shadows cast no spell,
where then is beauty going to dwell?
It dwells in us, a natural source,
resides in nature as a force.

57. A Willow Tree

A willow tree bends down to me
    beside a flowing stream;
the leaves and branches that I see
    bow down as in a dream.

How elegant these branches bow,
    as if to be in prayer,
and breezes whispering avow,
    "The willows beauty share."

I marveled at a wafting breeze
    that all the branches swayed,
as nature's offering to please,
    its charming show displayed.

58. Nature's Art

The leaves with burnished amber sheen
    flood hillsides, valleys with a glow,
as if in sunlight flames were seen,
    one huge mysterious flambeau.

How can it be that simple leaves
    become a magic work of art,
for one who sees this art believes
    its magic can transform the heart.

59. Nature's Prayer Shawl

Red leaves aglow from bright sun rays
    cast reddened shadows on the ground.
The dancing shadows seem ablaze;
    imaginary flames abound.

Nearby a yellow-leafed oak tree
    seems laden with bright coins of gold.
As sun beams paint each leaf I see,
    what glorious colors I behold.

How numerous the colors all
    that Mother Nature now gives birth,
creation's wonderful prayer shawl
    to shape our thanks through all the earth.

60. Nature's Icons

The landscape flows in gentle hills
that wait the blooming daffodils
of springtime with its thousand thrills.

They bloom along each country road
as flowers growing wild explode,
and winter's temperatures are slowed.

For now the pristine meadows beam
with sunlight that to us would seem
essential to the natural scheme

of daylight that a landscape paints
to which the moonlight adds restraints,
yet seems to be the work of saints,

who nature's icons shape in space,
as if designed to have their place
that through eternity we trace.

61. Colored Fantasy

Some red leaves peaked out from pine green,
and yellow, orange ones I've seen,
all paint another autumn scene.

The sunlight danced from leaf to leaf;
each dance was elegant but brief,
such beauty seemed beyond belief.

The tree limbs, a corps de ballet,
with costumed colors on display,
danced waltzes, fox trots, ev'n reggae,

as windblown orchestrations shaped
the dances that no leaf escaped;
some gold ones o'er an arbor draped.

O world of colored fantasy
that autumn each year brings to me,
your beauty shapes reality.

62. Beauty's Abode

Through winding roads and rolling hills
    I travel at slow speed
to drink in nature's hidden thrills,
    where beauty's guaranteed.

With every turn a crooked road
    reveals a different view.
Each one's a nature episode,
    a story ever new.

Around one turn I see a deer
    and then a long, red fox.
But cautiously I have to peer
    or land on roadside rocks.

The countryside is full of charm
    as leaves begin to turn.
Their colors worries can disarm,
    for such a time I yearn.

So travel on a winding road
    along a mountain side.
For beauty there has its abode
    on every hillside.

63. Nature's Balladeer

The wind sweeps through the barren trees
    with gentle, lilting sounds.
But it is not from rustling leaves,
    that lie, all piled in mounds.
The long, thin limbs like guitar strings
    vibrate with sound on sound,
as Mother Nature's music sings,
    and circles round and round.

The forest wind a symphony
    of windswept sounds creates;
it's not a harsh cacophony,
    but soft tunes generates.
Then hour by hour until the dawn,
    amazing sounds I hear,
until the wind dies and they're gone.
    Sweet nature's balladeer.

64. Nighttime Skies

When starlight fills the nighttime skies,
at times it's veiled by clouds' disguise,
which also covers moonbeam glow,
perhaps in winter veiled by snow.
But when the clouds are drawn away
by winds, we see the Milky Way;
we see Orion and Pisces,
or Leo, Virgo, and Aries.

The night sky is a panoply
of constellations' ecstasy.
And all at once a shooting star
expands the heav'ns' vast repertoire,
a repertoire of planets, moons
and stars evoking lovers' swoons.
A thing of wonder to delight
creation's glory every night.

Section 6

Nature's Care

65. Caring for Nature

The morning with sunrise begins,
    as moon and stars depart.
The sky a vast blue color wins
    and birds their courses start.

Canadian geese fly south in flocks
    that form a giant "V."
And as I stroll I see a fox
    behind a large oak tree.

The freshness of the morning air
    invigorates my soul
and frees it from the weight of care.
    How nature can console!

At noon under the sun's bright rays,
    the shade of an elm tree
protects me on the hottest days,
    lest I should be carefree.

How interesting that nature cares
    for me, as I should care
for nature, yet I create snares
    that nature can impair.

As morning sunrise and fresh air
    are nature's gifts to me,
I pray I will for nature care
    the way it cares for me:

to stop pollution, fracking too,
    help neighbors, friends to see
strip-mining from a different view,
    rivers pollution free!

66. Nature's Final Curtain Call

What if all nature slowly dies
and beauty cannot grace your eyes?
What if the rivers overrun
with damage in the millions done?
What if earth's temperatures should rise
to heights beyond human surprise,
and flora, fauna are extinct,
and all to global warming linked?
If wonder, beauty are not there
and nature's splendors we can't share,
with awe stripped from the human soul,
what will be left to make us whole?
A flower's fragrance would be lost;
there's no more snow and no more frost.
You could not to your love propose
while offering a bright red rose.
An orchard would be bare of trees,
and crops would vanish by degrees.
The barrenness around the globe
would seem to be death's shroud or robe.
What will then humankind befall
at nature's final curtain call?

67. Nature's Misuse

The earth in cycles has a time
    to each its special gifts to bring.
And wonders happen in each clime,
    in summer, autumn, winter, spring.

A desert flower peeks through sand,
    and salmon come back from the sea.
As acorns, seeds fall on the land;
    new plants will grow, perhaps a tree.

In nature unique times are set
    as all creation is reborn.
As seasons change, one can't forget
    first comes the blade, the ear, the corn.

Yet nature's cycles are disturbed
    through misused science and through greed
One pleads, "This misuse must be curbed,
    the ozone layer dare not bleed

from greenhouse gases undue strain
    upon the fragile atmosphere."
Most climate changes they explain,
    though doubters claim they don't appear.

But follow science and you'll learn
> how desperate the current need
to make a quick, sharp about-turn
> to save our planet from vile greed.

One knows the industries at fault,
> the ones producing greenhouse gas,
and while their profits they exalt,
> earth's nature's suffering en masse.

68. New Jersey Beaches, Past and Present

The trash along the broad shoreline,
    a frightful sight to see,
where crabs were trapped by fishing line
    and piles of gross debris,
gave one a sickening feeling that
    the ocean was quite ill,
without a decent habitat
    for shrimp, or crab, or krill.

Just one short walk along the shore
    and more of this you saw.
The plastic bottles more and more:
    pollute, defy the law.
And nature's pebbles and white sand
    were in a swift demise.
Wherever that you placed your hand,
    you sensed the shoreline dies.

When years ago we watched at night
    the ships dump, burn their trash,
it seemed we saw the sunset's light,
    but beaches filled with ash.
The ashes floated to the shore
    from ships that garbage dumped.
And then the giant cleanup chore
    left all the critics stumped.

The states, New Jersey and New York,
    now have much stricter laws,
and heavier fines the courts uncork
    to stop pollution's cause.
A fifty-thousand-dollar fine
    is for a first offense
for dumping, courts today assign;
    it's ocean's just defense.

69. The Holy Ganges?

For miles the Ganges River runs
    from Himalayan heights
through giant cities, little ones,
    adorned with sacred sights.
"This river's holy," claim Hindus,
    "endowed with sacred power."
Yet people, industry misuse
    this river hour by hour.

Both human and industrial waste
    replace this river's fame:
"most holy" now is "most disgraced,"
    pollution is to blame.
It spreads disease and causes death
    to thousands year by year.
The stench so great that with each breath,
    there's illness, death to fear.

There's now contaminated land
    where farmers can't grow crops,
and air pollution is at hand,
    which human labor stops.
Contaminated water, food,
    the Ganges is the source.
Thus "holy water" does no good;
    it is a deadly force.

70. Out of Control

The lightning, thunder, hail, and rain
light up and strike my window pane.
The crash and clatter both resound,
as bolts of lightning strike the ground.
The grass is singed and turned dark black,
while large booms sound like an attack
of bombs descending from the sky,
yet Mother Nature can't say why.
Such storms as these are here quite rare,
but global warming lays them bare.
If winter storms come in the fall,
it seems there's no control at all.
If summer storms come in the spring,
tornadoes wipe out everything.
Sea water's warmer by degrees,
and winds entire towns swiftly seize.
With fossil fuels oceans rise,
and island nature slowly dies.

71. The Earth on Fire

The temperatures are on the rise
    as forest fires expand.
The soil is dry, it's no surprise
    that fires destroy the land.

The fires are primed by increased drought,
    by dry soil, shrubs, and trees;
and climate change there is no doubt,
    destroys, kills by degrees.

The rising ocean temperature,
    the reason and the cause,
why salmon population's sure
    its migration will pause.

They need cold water to migrate,
    their young to spawn and hatch,
but climate change can change their fate,
    for it they are no match.

Pine beetles in dry climates thrive
    and weaken, kill the trees;
prime fuels on which fires survive
    just burn, and burn with ease.

As fires increase, the stifling threat
    by humans must be checked,
or else destruction they abet,
    and forests will be wrecked!

72. Though Winter, It's Like Springtime

Though winter, it's like springtime,
    but trees are not in bloom.
How pleasant! What a warm clime
    from New York to Khartoum.

But this cannot be normal,
    their climates aren't the same,
and this is quite abnormal,
    though some reject this claim!

Of global warming reason
    is not the major cause,
for when we lose a season,
    we bypass nature's laws.

This breach of Mother Nature
    now shortens earthly life;
we have no nomenclature
    that's equal to this strife.

The horror of our action,
    destructive, it is this:
we're left with no distraction;
    we know what time it is!

It's late, yes, almost too late
    to change this deadly course,
but nations now must create
    new green laws they enforce!

73. Ignorance We Can't Afford

In Africa parched, cracking ground
    has seen no rain for months on end,
and starving animals are found
    as hunger, drought, death's fate extend.

When nature's cycles are disturbed,
    that farmers know a harvest bring,
then violations go uncurbed
    from which the greenhouse gases spring.

There's much too much of CO_2
    from fossil fuels constant use,
and fracking methods are a clue
    to excess methane gas abuse.

"Let science-data be ignored,"
    some politicians boldly say.
Such ignorance we can't afford,
    and nature's desperate needs betray.

74. An Estuary

An estuary's widened mouth,
    where ocean tides and rivers meet,
is filled in east, west, north, and south
    with ecosystems incomplete.
Freshwater and saltwater merge
    each day with every rise of tide.
Saltwater flows in with a surge
    where swimmers and where surfers ride.

The estuaries protect land
    from crashing waves and violent storms.
They filter runoff, though unplanned,
    and create ecosystem norms:
the unique animals and plants,
    adapting to the brackish scene,
provide food, sustenance perchance,
    and help keep landscapes, water clean.

Industrial, dreadful pollution
    can be the awful, drastic cause
of damage without solution
    and without population's pause.
Some coastal watersheds are drained,
    some suffer from overfishing.
Can populations now be trained
    for *doing* instead of *wishing*?

75. "Creation's Care"

"Creation's care!" a vital cry:
    caress the earth, the forests, trees.
By no means let the oceans die,
    or island folk bring to their knees.

"Creation's care" should now become
    a topic of our daily speech
reminding us how careless, dumb
    to place such care beyond all reach.

"Creation's care," no hopeless task,
    no futile gesture from the left,
our negligence it will unmask,
    lest we're of nature's gifts bereft.

"Creation's care" takes effort, work
    "Creation's care," each day's concern,
no person can afford to shirk.
    "Creation's care" we all must learn.

www.ingramcontent.com/pod-product-compliance
Lightning Source LLC
LaVergne TN
LVHW051135080426
835510LV00018B/2422